T0080454

Wolfgang Amadeus Mozart
Symphony No. 35 in D major / D-Dur
K385 'Haffner'

Edited by / Herausgegeben von
Harry Newstone

EULENBURG

EAS 149
ISBN 978-3-7957-6549-1
ISMN M-2002-2373-6

© 2007 Ernst Eulenburg & Co GmbH, Mainz
for Europe excluding the British Isles
Ernst Eulenburg Ltd, London
for all other countries
Edition based on Eulenburg Study Score ETP 437
CD ℗ & © 1989 Naxos Rights International Ltd

Ernst Eulenburg Ltd
48 Great Marlborough Street
London W1F 7BB

Contents / Inhalt

Preface

Composed: late-July 1782 in Vienna
First performed: early-August 1782 in Salzburg, on the occasion
of the ennoblement of Sigmund Haffner
Original publisher: Artaria, Vienna, 1785
Versions: the work was originally a serenade in 6 movements: a March
initially preceded the Allegro; there was a second minuet in addition to the
one that remains; there were no parts for flutes or clarinets. Presented here,
however, is only the (4-movement) symphony version, which Mozart first
performed in March 1783 in one of his Academy Concerts in Vienna
Orchestration: 2 flutes, 2 oboes, 2 clarinets, 2 bassoons – 2 horns,
2 trumpets – timpani – strings
Duration: ca. 17 minutes

The summer of 1782 was an extraordinarily busy time for Mozart. His opera *Die Entführung aus dem Serail* was given its first performance on 16 July at the Burgtheater, Vienna, and he immediately began to work on an arrangement of it for winds: 'If I don't', he wrote to his father on 20 July, 'someone will anticipate me and secure the profits. And now you ask me to write a new symphony!'

The complaint was in response to a letter from Leopold asking for a new work to celebrate the coming ennoblement of Wolfgang's boyhood friend, Sigmund Haffner (1756–1787), for whose family he had written the now famous March (K249) and Serenade (K250) exactly six years earlier. Now, on top of everything else, Wolfgang was planning his own wedding (strongly opposed by Leopold) to Constanze Weber on 4 August. Exactly what it was that his father had asked for is uncertain for Leopold's letter is now lost. Wolfgang refers to it as a 'symphony' and, ever dutiful, he immediately began to work on what was to become another six-movement serenade – a march, an *Allegro*, an *Andante* flanked by two minuets and a *Presto* Finale. In his letter of 20 July he continues: 'You may rely on having something from me by every post. I shall work as fast as possible and, as far as haste permits, I shall turn out good work.' The composition did not, however, proceed as quickly as he had hoped and on 27 July he wrote to his father: 'You will be surprised and disappointed to find that this contains only the first *Allegro*; but it has been quite impossible to do more for you, for I have had to compose in a great hurry a serenade, but only for wind-instruments (otherwise I could have used it for you too). On Wednesday the 31ˢᵗ I shall send the two minuets, the *Andante* and the last movement. If I can manage to do so, I shall send a march too. If not, you will just have to use the one [K249] in the Haffner music [K250], which hardly anyone knows.'

On 31 July Wolfgang apologises again for the delay in the completion of the work – Sigmund's ennoblement had already taken place two days earlier. 'You see that my intentions are good – only what one cannot do one cannot! I am really unable to scribble off inferior stuff. So I cannot send you the whole symphony until next post-day.'

On 7 August Mozart wrote to Leopold: 'I send you herewith a short march [K408/2]. I only hope that all will reach you in good time, and be to your taste. The first *Allegro* must be played with great fire, the last – as fast as possible.'

Presumably the two minuets, the *Andante* and the Finale had been dispatched in the meantime but neither a covering letter from Mozart nor an acknowledgement from his father have survived. Neither has the letter from Leopold describing the festivities surrounding Sigmund Haffner's ennoblement which would have helped to establish when the symphony was played in Salzburg, but a date around the middle of August might be conjectured since on 24 August Wolfgang wrote to his father: 'I am delighted that the symphony is to your taste'.

Four months later, on 21 December, Mozart wrote to Leopold: 'You must know that I replied to your last letter on 4th December and expected an answer from you in eight days. Nothing came. […] I also asked you to send me by the first opportunity which presents itself the new symphony which I composed for Haffner at your request. I should like to have it for certain before Lent, for I should very much like to have it performed at my concert.'

Leopold was uncharacteristically slow in complying with Wolfgang's request and it was not until February, after a number of reminders, that the score arrived in Vienna. In his letter of acknowledgement, dated 15 February 1783, Mozart writes: 'My new Haffner symphony has positively amazed me, for I had forgotten every single note of it. It must surely produce a good effect.'

On receiving the score Mozart discarded the march and one of the minuets and added 2 flutes and 2 clarinets to the first and last movements by writing them in respectively on the blank top and bottom staves of the score. He also crossed out the first movement repeat bar which faces both ways at the end of the exposition although there is no corresponding repeat bar at the end of the movement. The added flute and clarinet parts have only a single barline at the end of the exposition.

The Lenten Academy (given for Mozart's benefit) at which the new Haffner Symphony was first played in Vienna took place at the Burgtheater on 23 March. On 29 March Mozart sent his father an account of the evening: 'I need not tell you very much about the success of my concert, for no doubt you have already heard of it. Suffice it to say that the theatre could not have been more crowded and that every box was full. But what pleased me most of all was that His Majesty the Emperor was present and, goodness! – how delighted he was and how he applauded me!' There follows details of the programme which began with 'The new

Haffner Symphony' and ended with its last movement, between which was a miscellany of assorted works by Mozart (arias, concertos, variations and a short solo fugue 'because the Emperor was present').

The 'Haffner' Symphony was first published in Vienna in 1785 by Artaria, and also in Paris where it was played at the Concert Spirituel for whom Mozart had composed the Symphony in D major, K297, in 1778. The 'Haffner' Symphony with its opening *premier coup d'archet* must have delighted the Parisian audience just as this device (a forceful unison attack by the full orchestra) had done when Mozart – with his eye on Parisian taste – used it in the 'Paris' Symphony. To this day the 'Haffner' Symphony has remained one of the composer's most popular and often played works.

Harry Newstone

Vorwort

Komponiert: Ende Juli 1782 in Wien
Uraufführung: Anfang August 1782 in Salzburg, anlässlich Sigmund
Haffners Erhebung in den Adelsstand
Originalverlag: Artaria, Wien, 1785
Fassungen: Ursprünglich war das Werk eine Serenade in 6 Sätzen:
Dem Allegro ging eine Marcia voraus und außer dem erhaltenen
gab es ein zweites Menuett. Flöten und Klarinetten fehlten.
Überliefert ist jedoch nur die (viersätzige) Sinfonie-Fassung, die Mozart
erstmals im Marz 1783 in einer seiner Wiener Akademien aufführte.
Orchesterbesetzung: 2 Flöten, 2 Oboen, 2 Klarinetten, 2 Fagotte –
2 Hörner, 2 Trompeten – Pauken – Streicher
Spieldauer: etwa 17 Minuten

Im Sommer 1782 hatte Mozart außerordentlich viel zu tun. Seine Oper *Die Entführung aus dem Serail* wurde am 16. Juli am Wiener Burgtheater uraufgeführt. Sofort danach begann Mozart mit einer Bearbeitung der Oper für Bläser: „sonst kommt mir einer bevor – und hat anstatt meiner den Profit davon; und soll nun eine Neue Sinphonie auch machen!", schrieb er am 20. Juli an seinen Vater.

Die Beschwerde bezog sich auf die brieflich geäußerte Bitte Leopolds um ein neues Werk für die Feier zur Erhebung von Wolfgangs Jugendfreund Sigmund Haffner (1756–1787) in den Adelsstand. Für die Haffner-Familie hatte Mozart genau sechs Jahre zuvor schon den mittlerweile berühmten Marsch (KV 249) und die Serenade (KV 250) geschrieben. Als hätte Wolfgang nicht schon genug zu tun, plante er darüber hinaus auch noch seine eigene Hochzeit mit Constanze Weber am 4. August (womit er auf starken Widerstand Leopolds stieß). Man weiß nicht genau, was für eine Komposition sich Leopold erbeten hatte, da sein Brief nicht mehr existiert. Wolfgang nannte sie eine „Sinphonie", und pflichtbewusst wie immer begann er sofort mit der Arbeit an einem Werk, das sich als eine weitere sechssätzige Serenade herausstellen sollte – ein Marsch, ein *Allegro*, ein von zwei Menuetten umrahmtes *Andante* und ein *Presto*-Schlusssatz. In seinem Brief vom 20. Juli fuhr Mozart fort: „sie sollen alle Postage sicher etwas bekommen – und ich werde soviel möglich geschwind arbeiten – und so viel es die Eile zulässt – gut schreiben". Die Arbeit an der Komposition ging allerdings nicht so schnell voran wie erhofft und am 27. Juli schrieb Wolfgang an seinen Vater: „Sie werden augen machen, daß sie nur das Erste Allegro sehen; allein – es war nicht anderst möglich – ich habe geschwind eine Nacht Musique machen müssen, aber nur auf harmonie, (sonst hätte ich sie für *Sie* auch brauchen können) – Mittwoch den 31:^{ten} schicke ich die zwei Menuett das Andante und lezte Stück – kann ich – so schicke auch einen Marche – wo nicht so müssen Sie halt den [KV 249] von der Hafner Musique [KV 250] (der *sehr* unbekannt ist) machen."

Am 31. Juli entschuldigte sich Mozart wiederum wegen der Verzögerung beim Abschluss der Komposition – Sigmunds Erhebung in den Adelsstand hatte schon zwei Tage zuvor stattgefunden. „Sie sehen, daß der Willen gut ist; allein wenn man nicht kann, so kann man nicht! – ich mag nichts hinschmiren. – ich kann ihnen also erst künftigen Postage die ganze Sinphonie schicken."

Am 7. August schrieb Mozart an Leopold: „Hier schicke ich ihnen einen kurzen marsch! [KV 408/2] – Wünsche nur das noch alles zur rechten zeit kommen möchte – und nach ihrem geschmack seye. – das Erste Allegro muß recht feüerig gehen. – das lezte – so geschwind als es möglich ist."

Wahrscheinlich hatte Mozart die zwei Menuette, das *Andante* und den Schlusssatz schon vorher geschickt, aber weder ein Begleitbrief von ihm noch eine Bestätigung des Erhalts von seinem Vater wurden überliefert. Auch existiert der Brief von Leopold nicht mehr, in dem jener die Feierlichkeiten zur Adelung Sigmund Haffners beschrieb. Dieser Brief hätte Aufschlüsse geben können, wann die Sinfonie in Salzburg gespielt wurde. Man kann allerdings annehmen, dass sie Mitte August zur Aufführung kam, denn am 24. August schrieb Wolfgang an seinen Vater: „mich freuet es recht sehr daß die Sinphonie nach ihrem geschmack ausgefallen ist."

Vier Monate später, am 21. Dezember, schrieb Mozart an Leopold: „Sie müssen wissen daß ich auf ihr leztes schreiben den 4ten Dezem:^{bre} geantwortet habe; folglich in 8 tägen antwort erwartet habe – es kamm nichts; [...] und daß wenn sie eine gelegenheit finden, Sie die güte haben möchten mir die *Neue Sinfonie* die ich ihnen für den Hafner geschrieben, zu schicken; wenn ich sie nur bis fasten gewiss habe, denn ich möchte sie gerne in meiner academic machen."

Leopold nahm sich ungewöhnlich viel Zeit bei der Erfüllung von Mozarts Bitte. Erst im Februar, nach einer Reihe von Mahnungen, kam die Partitur in Wien an. In Mozarts Brief vom 15. Februar 1783, in dem jener den Erhalt bestätigte, steht: „die neue Hafner Sinfonie hat mich ganz surprenirt – dann ich wusste kein Wort mehr davon; – die muß gewiss guten Effekt machen."

Nach dem Erhalt der Partitur strich Mozart den Marsch und eines der Menuette und fügte zwei Flöten und zwei Klarinetten zum ersten und letzten Satz hinzu, indem er ihre Stimmen jeweils in die ungenutzten obersten und untersten Notensysteme der Partitur eintrug. Im ersten Satz strich er zudem die in beide Richtungen zeigenden Wiederholungszeichen am Ende der Exposition. Das entsprechende Wiederholungszeichen am Ende des Satzes fehlt ohnehin. Die hinzugefügten Flöten und Klarinettenstimmen haben nur einen einfachen Taktstrich am Ende der Exposition.

Die in der Fastenzeit veranstaltete Akademie, ausschließlich mit Werken von Mozart, in der die neue *Haffner*-Sinfonie erstmals in Wien gespielt wurde, fand am 23. März im Burgtheater statt. Am 29. März schickte Mozart seinem Vater einen Bericht über den Abend: „Ich glaube es wird nicht nöthig seyn ihnen viel von dem erfolg meiner academie zu schreiben, sie werden es vieleicht schon gehört haben. genug; das theater hätte ohnmöglich völler seyn können, und alle logen waren besezt. – das liebste aber war mir, daß seine Mayestätt der kayser auch zugegen war, und wie vergnügt er war, und was für lauten beyfall er mir gegeben." Dann folgen im Brief Einzelheiten über das Programm, das mit der neuen „Hafner Simphonie" begann und mit ihrem letzten Satz endete. Dazwischen hatte man eine Reihe diverser Mozart-Stücke eingeschoben (Arien, Konzerte, Variationen und eine kurze Solofuge, „weil der kayser da war").

Die *Haffner*-Sinfonie wurde erstmals 1785 bei Artaria in Wien veröffentlicht und auch in Paris, wo sie in einem *Concert spirituel* zur Aufführung gelangte, eine Konzertreihe, für die Mozart schon 1778 die Sinfonie in D-Dur, KV 297 komponiert hatte. Die *Haffner*-Sinfonie mit ihrem *premier coup d'archet* (kraftvollen Einsatz des gesamten Orchesters im Unisono) wurde vom Pariser Publikum bestimmt genauso begeistert aufgenommen wie ehedem die *Pariser* Sinfonie, in der sich Mozart schon einmal dieses Kunstgriffs – mit einem Auge auf den Pariser Geschmack – bedient hatte. Noch heute ist die *Haffner*-Sinfonie eines der beliebtesten und am häufigsten gespielten Werke des Komponisten.

Harry Newstone
Übersetzung: Elke Hockings

Symphony No. 35

Wolfgang Amadeus Mozart
(1756–1791)
K385

I. Allegro con spirito

EAS 149

© 2007 Ernst Eulenburg Ltd, London
and Ernst Eulenburg & Co GmbH, Mainz

4

38

42

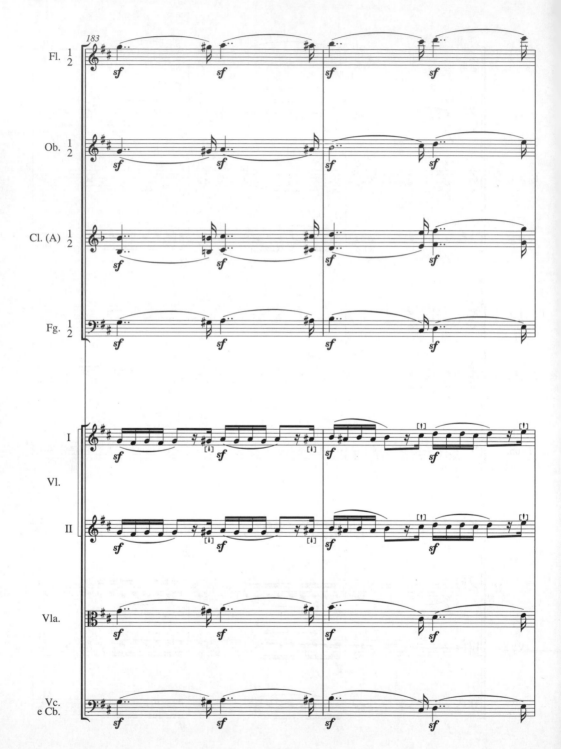

II. Andante

58

III. Menuetto

Trio

Menuetto da capo

IV. Presto

94

EAS 149

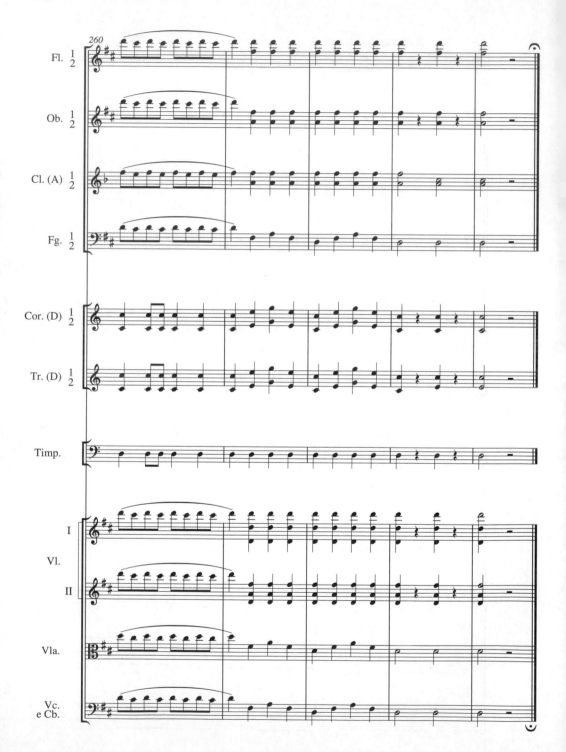

Printed in China